2

The Lipizzaners

ALOIS PODHAJSKY

THE LIPIZZANERS

Translated by
EVA PODHAJSKY

GEORGE G. HARRAP & CO. LTD
London · Toronto · Wellington · Sydney

Photo Credits

Tony Armstrong-Jones (Agency Schweitzer-Hecht, Munich) (Plates 33, 160, 174) — Barratts Photo Press, London (Plate 108) — Brüder Basch, Vienna (Plates 107, 152) — Robert A. E. Bauer, Salzburg (Plate 9) — Heinrich von der Becke, Berlin (Plate 49) — Charles J. Belden, St. Petersburg (Florida) (Plates 15, 124, 125) — Dierks, Basel (Plate 58) — Fritz Eicher, Thun (Plate 123) — Gustav J. Essinger, Frankfurt (Plate 70) — Frankenstein, Vienna (Plate 120) — Heinrich Grauer, Vienna (Plate 175) — Hoffenreich, Vienna (Plates 151, 153) — Hans Hammarskiöld, Stockholm (Plate 113) — Conrad Horster, Cologne (Plate 72) — Theodor Janssen, Kalkum bei Düsseldorf (Plates 133, 156) — Fritz Kern, Vienna (Plates 23, 24, 25, 26, 27, 28, 29, 30, 31, 32, 35, 40, 54, 56, 57, 62, 65, 71, 74, 96, 101, 105, 117, 147, 161, 163, 164, 165, 167, 172, 173) — Bruno Kerschner, Salzburg (Plates 64, 102, 104, 110) — Keystone Press Agency, Vienna (Plates 92, 157) — Herbert Kofler, Vienna (Plates 39, 140) — Michael Kössler, Vienna (Plates 51, 55, 82, 98) — Life Photo, New York (Plate 128) — Mateo, Barcelona (Plate 136) — Werner Menzendorf, Berlin (Plates 3, 4, 5, 7, 10, 11, 12, 13, 14, 18, 21, 22, 36, 37, 38, 41, 43, 48, 50, 52, 53, 63, 66, 67, 73, 77, 78, 79, 80, 81, 90, 93, 94, 112, 118, 127, 141, 142, 149, 150, 154, 155, 158) — Carl Pospesch, Salzburg (Plate 122) — Publifoto, Rome (Plate 126) — Relang, Vienna (Plate 119) — Reportagebild, Stockholm (Plates 106, 130) — Lothar Rübelt, Vienna (Plates 34, 47, 68, 115, 137) — Sport and General Press, London (Plate 134) — Ullstein, Berlin (Plate 44) — Usis-Photo, Vienna (Plates 6, 8, 97, 166, 168, 169, 170) — Harry Weber, Vienna (Plates 103, 116) — Guido Wedding, Essen (Plate 45) — Winkler, Vienna (Plates 145, 159) — Hildegard Zeuner (Plate 17).

Published originally under the title
"Die Lipizzaner im Bild"
by Nymphenburger Verlagshandlung

First published in Great Britain 1969
by GEORGE G. HARRAP & CO. LTD
182 High Holborn, London, W.C. I

SBN 245 59893 6

Printed in Germany

The Lipizzaners

Introduction

Lipizzaner is a magic word for any horseman and for everyone who loves animals and admires art and beauty. Their miraculous escape and survival during the chaos of the Second World War and their performances in many countries of Europe and in the United States and Canada have made the name of these horses known throughout the whole world. No wonder that every bit of news regarding this breed is received with great interest everywhere. But very often the enthusiast overlooks the fact that not every Lipizzaner is a member of the "dancing white horses" of the Spanish Riding School in Vienna, and that not every white horse is necessarily a Lipizzaner.

It is not the purpose of the present book to record the history of the Lipizzaners, which has already been set forth in my autobiography, "My Dancing White Horses." The reason for this book is to assemble the numerous photographs that have appeared in the above-mentioned book and in the three that followed—namely, "The White Stallions of Vienna," "The Complete Training of Horse and Rider," and "My Horses, My Teachers." These photographs will introduce new horse-lovers to the oldest breed in Europe, and also serve, I hope, as a graphic summary of its qualities and achievements.

The photographs of these powerful horses, taken at various stages of their lives, reveal their graceful movements and the absolute control of their muscles which readily suggest a comparison with the classical ballet. This comparison becomes even more pertinent in view of the fact that ballet and classical riding employ the same terms and expressions for the various figures and exercises. Indeed, horse "ballets" were much in favour at the royal courts of the seventeenth and eighteenth centuries. Although the Lipizzaner has become known throughout the world, there are different opinions about his origin. Let us, therefore, explain briefly the development of this breed.

For many centuries the Spanish horse—a crossing of Arab and Berber stallions with Andalusian mares—was of the same importance in Europe as the English

Thoroughbred is today. When the Moors were driven out of Spain, breeding which had reached a very high standard during their seven hundred years' reign gradually declined. In the following years attempts were made to continue the Spanish breed in various countries of Europe. So the Imperial court in Vienna ordered stallions and mares to be bought in Spain and transported to Lipizza, a small village near Trieste. Here the Imperial stud farm was founded in 1580 to make a new home for the Spanish horse, whose breeding was continued on the same principles. The horses born at this new stud farm were named Lipizzaners. Besides going to Lipizza, the Spanish horse was transplanted to many other parts of the Austrian Monarchy and was also bred in the royal stud farms of Denmark and Germany. Of all these ancient breeding farms only the stud farm of Lipizza has been preserved up to the present day, while many other similar stud farms have ceased to exist in the course of the centuries.

Although in the beginning Lipizza was founded for the purpose of furnishing the necessary horses for the Imperial mews in Vienna, the newly established breed exercised a considerable influence on horse-breeding in general in the Austro-Hungarian Empire and developed peacefully for the first two hundred years. Without any harm it lived through the more difficult and stormy times later in history—through the Napoleonic wars and the break-down of the Austro-Hungarian Monarchy in 1918. After the First World War Lipizza became Italian territory and Italy was allotted half of the original stock. The breeding of the Lipizzaners was continued according to tradition and was also maintained unchanged when, after the Second World War, this area was given to the state of Yugoslavia. It was at this moment that the stud farm was renamed Lipica. There had been a number of small Lipizzaner stud farms in this country before because in 1918 the newly established nation of Yugoslavia had taken rural horse-breeding over from the Austrian Empire and that breeding was strongly influenced by the Lipizzaners.

The other half of the Imperial stud farm, which had been allotted to Austria, was taken to Piber in Styria in 1919. From then on it was the task of this village in the mountains in the south of Austria to provide the necessary horses for the Spanish Riding School in Vienna. Formerly a property of the Imperial court, the School was placed under the control of the Republic of Austria, which then had become a very small country. All stallions at the Spanish Riding School come from the Federal stud farm in Piber and the School has had no contact whatsoever with Lipica or other government stud farms in Italy, Hungary, and Czechoslovakia which were also established with stock from Imperial breeding farms after the break-down of the Austro-Hungarian Empire, or with private breeding farms which have sprung up since in other countries.

According to the tradition observed at all stud farms, every Lipizzaner is branded at the age of six months. During the time of the Empire, only a horse born at the Imperial stud farm of Lipizza was branded with an L on his left cheek. Lipizzaners bred at other stud farms of the Austro-Hungarian Monarchy did not receive the L, although they, too, were called Lipizzaners. These horses were marked with symbols and numbers on their backs and with the brand of their stud farm on the left hindquarters. After 1918 the Italian authorities continued to apply the L on the left cheek as the only brand, just as had been the custom at the Imperial stud farm. In Hungary and Yugoslavia, also, the brands used on the Lipizzaners bred in those countries were maintained—for instance, in Yugoslavia it was a crown above letters or numbers on the left side of the back. From 1919 on the Lipizzaners bred in Piber were branded with an L on the left cheek. They are also marked with the brands of their origin on the back and with a crown above a P on the left hindquarters. All stallions trained at the Spanish Riding School are marked with this triple brand, thus carrying passport and pedigree.

The Lipizzaner breed of Austria which is the subject of this book and whose pictures have been gathered in this volume consists of six lines of stallions and eighteen families of mares. The stallion's double name is composed of his father's name preceding his mother's name. For instance, Maestoso Alea, Conversano Barbana, Neapolitano Santuzza, etc. This explains why the name of a stallion often sounds feminine, which may confuse the uninitiated.

LIST OF BRANDS

Father	Name	Mother
P	Pluto	〰
C	Conversano	∅
N	Neapolitano	⊁
F	Favory	▭
M	Maestoso	♔
S	Siglavy	⪪

If the sire of a foal springs from the Pluto line, the young Lipizzaner is marked with a P on his back. If his mother also descends from a Pluto stallion, the foal is branded with a wavy line, the symbol of the female Pluto origin. If his mother descends from, say, a Maestoso stallion, the second brand would be a crown, the symbol of the Maestoso line in mares. Thus with corresponding brands for the paternal and maternal lines every Lipizzaner's genealogy is clearly recorded.

Today the Lipizzaner is the very idea of a white horse, but—like most greys—he is born dark brown or charcoal grey. In the course of the years he becomes as white as his parents. Some young horses begin to turn grey at three years of age, others at seven or even later. The visitor to the stud farm is confronted with the strange sight of the snow-white mothers and their dark offspring grazing peacefully in the pastures. On very rare occasions one of these dark foals maintains his brown coat, so that now and again there is a bay stallion at the Spanish Riding School.

In the lush pastures of the stud farm of Piber the young Lipizzaner foal spends a carefree childhood protected by his mother who calmly watches his clumsy little leaps, in which, however, you may detect the trace of a capriole. The horses are taken into pastures in the early-morning hours and spend the hot part of the day and the cool nights in the spacious barns. The foal remains with his mother for six months and then enjoys unlimited freedom in the vast pastures together with other foals of his age.

At the end of their first year the yearlings are separated and gathered into herds of colts and fillies. From May to September they spend the summer in the Alps, 4,500 feet above sea-level. The fragrant grass and the hard soil give the Lipizzaner strength and endurance and make his legs clean and his hooves small and hard. This is the moment when the young horses begin to change colour; white hairs appear in their dark coats and in the black manes and tails—only a few to begin with, until gradually the coats become lighter and lighter. This process of changing varies according to the individual. In most cases the dark colour remains for a longer period on the legs or in mane and tail. In carefree and playful gaiety the young horses gallop up and down the mountainsides and measure their strength in friendly rough-and-tumble games. The young stallions, especially, enjoy these scuffles and carry them on endlessly until the game turns into serious fights and, later, many a scar gives evidence of these duels. This is the reason why in their third year the stallions may no longer remain in the pastures unattended.

Serious life begins for the young Lipizzaner stallion when at three and a half years of age he is taken to the Spanish Riding School in Vienna for his schooling. From now on there is no more recreation and relaxation in the pastures, for he will rarely ever leave the city again. Only in the years 1941 to 1944 were the School stallions taken for their summer holidays to the Lainzer Park on the outskirts of Vienna.

Those happy few who go back to the stud farm of Piber in order to fulfil their duty as sires are the only ones to see the green mountains again. The young mares are broken to a carriage at the stud farm and in a four-in-hand give evidence of the tradition of driving before joining, in turn, the herd of brood mares.

The forefather of the Lipizzaner, the Spanish horse, was mainly used and appreciated as a riding horse. But in the course of centuries his descendants have proved to be excellent carriage horses and were used as such in the Imperial mews at the court in Vienna. The Lipizzaner is by no means made only for the intricate movements of the classical high school. On the contrary, he is widely appreciated as a carriage horse and as a riding horse in general. One more proof of this fact was furnished by the Lipizzaner stallions in the years 1941 to 1944 when they were taken on unaccustomed cross-country rides in the Lainzer Park.

At the Spanish Riding School in Vienna the classical art of riding has been preserved in its purest form as it was handed down through the centuries. Moreover, the Lipizzaner stud farm is given the direction for breeding by the School, which in turn serves as a center of examination, for only those stallions who have proved their value at the Spanish Riding School will go back to the stud farm as sires to pass on their talents and abilities as well as their intelligence and good character.

When visiting this institution foreigners very often raise the question how and why there is a Spanish Riding School in Vienna, and often they will think that the art of riding practised here is of Spanish origin or that the name is derived from the ceremonial Spanish etiquette of the Habsburg court. The truth is that the name goes back to the Spanish horses that were first used when the riding school was founded. In the sixteenth century the classical art of riding was at its peak and riding academies were established at all royal courts of Europe. At the Imperial court of Vienna these Spanish horses were trained from about 1560 on in the "Spanish riding stables," that is, in the Spanish Riding School. This name, which pointed to the origin of the horses, was maintained even when, long afterwards, the Imperial stud farm of Lipizza provided the mounts for the Imperial family and the members of the court.

The training of the Lipizzaner stallion is long and carefully planned. At first the young stallion is made familiar with the change in his life. He has to become accustomed to spending his days in a stable. Bridling and saddling are new experiences just as are the various forms and movements that will be demanded from him later. It should never be overlooked that very highly bred and intelligent creatures make greater demands on the skill and the understanding of their teachers than less intelligent ones, and, therefore, require especially careful treatment. The first work is done on the longe, that is, the young horse moves on a long longe rein in a circle around his trainer. He should find his balance and acquire the first notions of guidance and obedience. Regular work strengthens his muscles and prepares him for the work under the rider whom he should carry willingly. The first year of training of the young Lipizzaner stallion is exactly the same as should be given to every good riding horse that is trained according to the classical principles. As the child has to acquire the basic knowledge in school before continuing to a higher education, the young stallion must begin by learning the three basic paces—walk, trot, and canter—and execute them in full balance. This is called the campaign and enables him to proceed to the more difficult training in which the demands are gradually increased. He must learn to understand the aids of his rider and become supple and obedient, concentrate entirely on his rider and not be distracted by anything. When he has mastered all the difficult exercises and is able to perform half passes, pirouettes, and flying changes with graceful ease, he has reached the stage of high school.

The high school or haute école is divided into the exercises or airs on the ground and the airs above the ground. While the exercises on the ground are demanded in the dressage test at the Olympic Games, the airs above the ground have become a relic of the past. Except in old paintings and etchings these traditional movements are preserved only by the Lipizzaner stallions of the Spanish Riding School, the last abode of the classical art of riding. Piaffe and passage count among the exercises on the ground. These graceful movements reveal the powerful stallion as a four-legged dancer. Piaffe is a trot on the spot, full of cadence and rhythm and reminding us of the classical ballet. In the passage the stallion floats above the ground in a solemn and proud movement, like a trot in slow motion, weightless and in absolute control of his muscles and sinews. It is a sight enjoyed by both experts and non-experts. With the perfection of piaffe and passage the dressage or, better, the gymnastic training of the stallion has reached the peak. When all the exercises and figures of the high school are performed on the curb only, all four reins held in the left hand, images of the brilliant times of the classical art of riding seem to come to new life. This is also the ultimate proof of the correct training of the horse.

So high an aim can be reached only by an intelligent course of training which is built up systematically and which allows the necessary space of time—just as with the classical ballet—and in which the demands are increased gradually. The Lipizzaner stallion is initiated to the piaffe in work in hand in which he learns these difficult steps. Work in the pillars may also increase and enhance the piaffe. At the same time it is in work in hand and between the pillars that the stallion reveals to his master for which of the airs above the ground—levade, courbette, ballotade, or capriole—he is especially gifted. This work requires great intuition and a gift of observation on the part of the trainer, for he must detect the talent of the stallion from the most insignificant signs and reactions. It should not be expected that the horse will reveal his talent right away by performing a perfect levade or capriole. When in the work in hand or between the pillars the trainer demands that the hindlegs of the horse step under his body in an increased measure so that the weight is taken off the forehand, a horse with a calm temperament will rise into a levade. Immediate reward will make him understand that he has reacted to the satisfaction of his teacher. The fact should be underlined that we may speak about a levade only when the stallion lowers his hindquarters with deeply bent joints. If he raises his forehand standing up on his stretched hindlegs he is merely rearing. When the stallion has understood the commands and is able to execute the levade in the manner described he will have little difficulty performing it with the weight of a rider on his back. The levade reminds us of numerous equestrian monuments, most vividly of all the monument of Prince Eugene of Savoy on the Heldenplatz in Vienna.

A stallion with a more ardent temperament will not allow himself to be retained in this rather uncomfortable position, which may be compared to a deep genuflection. After a moment he will try to rise on his hindlegs and even make a jump forward. The riding masters of the past centuries called this leap a croupade. When this leap on the hindlegs is repeated several times—two to eight times—we speak about a classical courbette. It is also taught in hand at first, and when it is well established it may be performed under the rider. Horse and rider combine their efforts to produce a bit of memorable art.

Sometimes a stallion is so full of temperament that the effort of a piaffe or a levade is beyond his self-control and he tries to evade the demanded exercise by leaping into the air with all four legs. This will lead to a ballotade or a capriole. We speak about a ballotade (palotade in the eighteenth century) when the stallion jumps into the air, his body horizontal to the ground, stretching his hindlegs only to the extent that the shoes are visible from behind. If he stretches his hindlegs to the utmost (the technical term is "striking"), he performs a capriole. This school jump may often be observed when colts at liberty in the pasture leap and gambol in their play. It was also an important manœuvre in medieval combat on horseback. By means of such a leap the encircled horseman tried to evade his enemies and by the power-ful striking of his horse's hindlegs kept them from pressing in on him.

When speaking about these spectacular school jumps which today are still practised at the Spanish Riding School, a short review of the history of this oldest riding academy of the world becomes pertinent. For many centuries this School lived through wars and revolutions without ever leaving the city of Vienna. At the end of the Second World War, however, for the first time in history the Lipizzaner stallions left the endangered city and in a miraculous flight in March, 1945, reached a small village in the west of Austria. Here, in St Martin in Upper Austria, on the 7th of May, 1945, occurred the historical performance by which the Lipizzaners succeeded in arousing the interest of the American Army commander General Patton. By their harmonious movements and their grace and beauty they gave weight to my request to rescue the Lipizzaner stud farm from Czechoslovakia where it had been taken against my will in 1942. General Patton had 234 Lipizzaners brought from Hostau back to Austria under military protection before the Russian troops reached that part of Czechoslovakia which had been designated as their zone of occupation. By this determined action of the general, the Spanish Riding School was saved from annihilation, for all the stallions that may be admired at the Spanish Riding School today are offsprings of those horses.

After the happy ending of the adventurous days of May, 1945, which may be called the second birthday of the Spanish Riding School, we had expected to be able to return to Vienna within a short time. But we were bitterly disappointed, for it was only in October, 1955, that this wish could be fulfilled. Ten years of exile were a very difficult time for the old institution. The standard of riding had to be main-tained at the required high level and our country itself had to be reminded of what a treasure it possessed. Performances in foreign countries were to re-establish the position of the Spanish Riding School in the horse world and make the time-honoured institution known everywhere. In the course of seven years the Spanish Riding School travelled to many countries of Europe, to the United States and Canada, and helped Austria to be esteemed as a country of old culture. In the difficult times of exile the Lipizzaners gave proof of their value when performing in many strange places and under difficult circumstances. And since their return to their home in October, 1955, visitors from all over the world have come to Vienna to see this equestrian ballet in its unique setting: in the Spanish Riding School which was built by Joseph Emanuel Fischer von Erlach in 1735 and which is without any doubt the most beautiful riding hall in the world.

The programme of the performance gives a precise idea of the training of the Lipiz-zaner from the time of the first schooling of the young stallions up to the work of the fully trained school stallion. The young generation is presented to the visitor in the group of young stallions with their partially dark coats. The school stallions appear in all paces and figures of the high school and in the Pas de Trois. The spectator witnesses work in hand and between the pillars, he sees the airs above the ground and a stallion on the long rein. In this section of the programme the school horse is guided by his master walking behind him and performs all the difficult exercises which he has learned before under the rider. The traditional closing of the performance is the great school quadrille which reminds us of the brilliant horse ballets of bygone days. The spectator falls under the spell of the graceful ease and the precise execution which are the result of systematic and conscientious training. The exact timing, the rhythmic and harmonious movements of the eight or twelve stallions in the quadrille, may well be called the peak of perfection of the classical art of riding. In his film, "The Miracle of the White Stallions" (1962) Walt Disney not only told the tale of the miraculous rescue of the Lipizzaners but also fashioned a monument to the Spanish Riding School.

This book will have accomplished its mission if it succeeds in making the reader familiar with the Lipizzaners and their performances at the Spanish Riding School and in underlining the role of these horses as the representatives of the traditional culture of the classical art of riding. These Lipizzaners are entitled to the greatest kindness and tender loving care in return for their unremitting willingness and co-operation. They deserve the fame and glory that have been bestowed upon them by generations of admirers. Mohammed's words seem to be written expressly for these horses:

Lipizzaners, you are indeed creatures without equal. You fly without wings and you conquer without swords!

1 *The three brood mares, Slavina, Dubovina II, and Allegra XVI, at feeding time. (Yugoslavian government stud farm Lipica [Lipizza], the former Imperial stud farm founded in 1580)*

2   *Brood mares and foals at the horse-pond at Lipizza*

3 *Since 1920 the Federal stud farm at Piber in Styria has provided the young horses for the Spanish Riding School*

4 In the morning the white mothers and their dark foals go out into the pastures . . .

5   ... *and return to their spacious stables in the evening*

6 *The stallion is master of the stud farm. Neapolitano Brenta in Piber*

Mother and son

8 *With much curiosity the yearlings watch everything that goes on around them*

9 One or other of the young Lipizzaners begins to turn grey before his brothers do

10   *In the summer the herds of the young horses are taken to the pastures in the high Alps*

11   *A proud descendant of an ancient bree*

12 *The favorite pastime of the young stallions is youthful play . . .*

14 Young Lipizzaner and Haflinger stallions on the Stubalp, which resembles somewhat the pastures of the original stud farm at Lipizza

15 *Safe from the chaos. The Lipizzaner stud farm in Wimsbach, Upper Austria*

16 *The stallions of the Spanish Riding School in their summer quarters in the Lainzer Park, Vienna*

17 The young mares are broken to a carriage

18 The tradition is continued at the stud farm of Piber and the mares are trained to a four-in-hand

19   In Lipizza stallions too are broken to a carriage. *Favory Sistina, Neapolitano Batosta XIII, Maestoso Allegra X, Neapolitano Mara VIII*

20 *The school stallions at the former Imperial residence in Lainz, 1941*

21 *The Lipizzaner proves to be a good cross-country horse*

22 *Cross-country in the Lainzer Park (1941 to 1944)*

23, 24 *At present the stallions are exercised during the holidays in the summer riding arena at the Imperial palace in Vienna*

25 *The two stars of the performance "On the long rein": Siglavy Monterosa . . .*

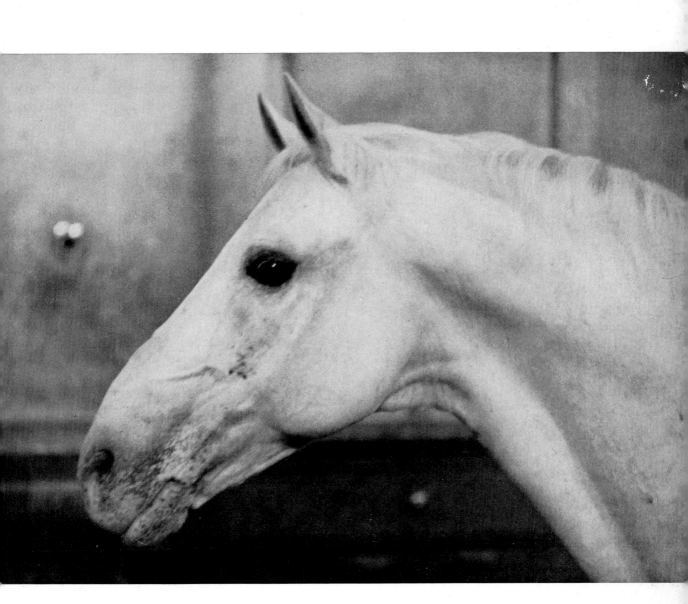

26 *. . . and his predecessor, Conversano Plutona*

28 *Daily grooming helps to establish confidence in man*

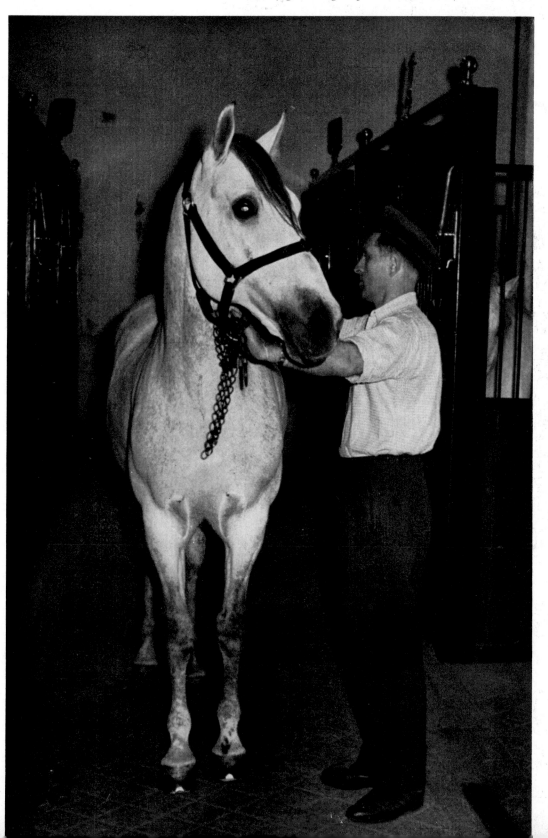

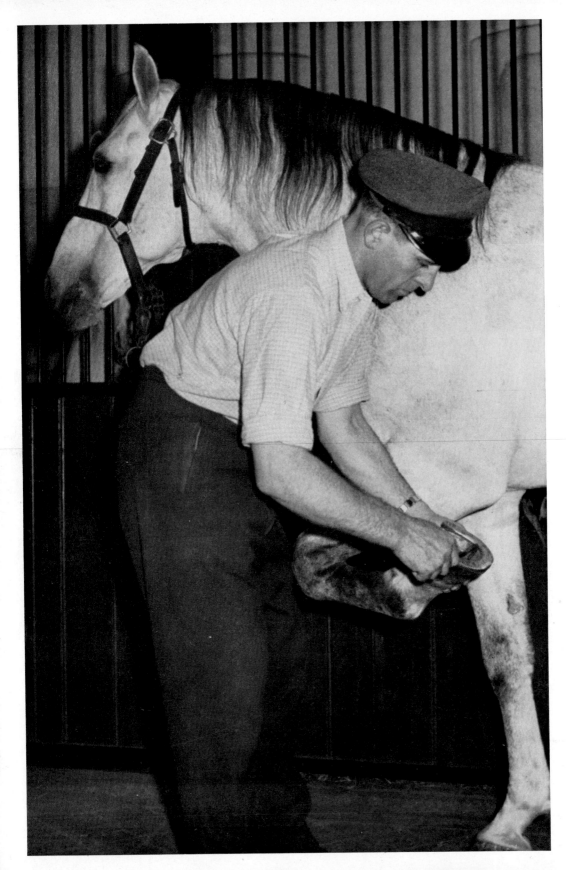

29 Correct shoeing
and hoof-care a
important for the
horse's health

The silky tail of
the Lipizzaner
demands special
care

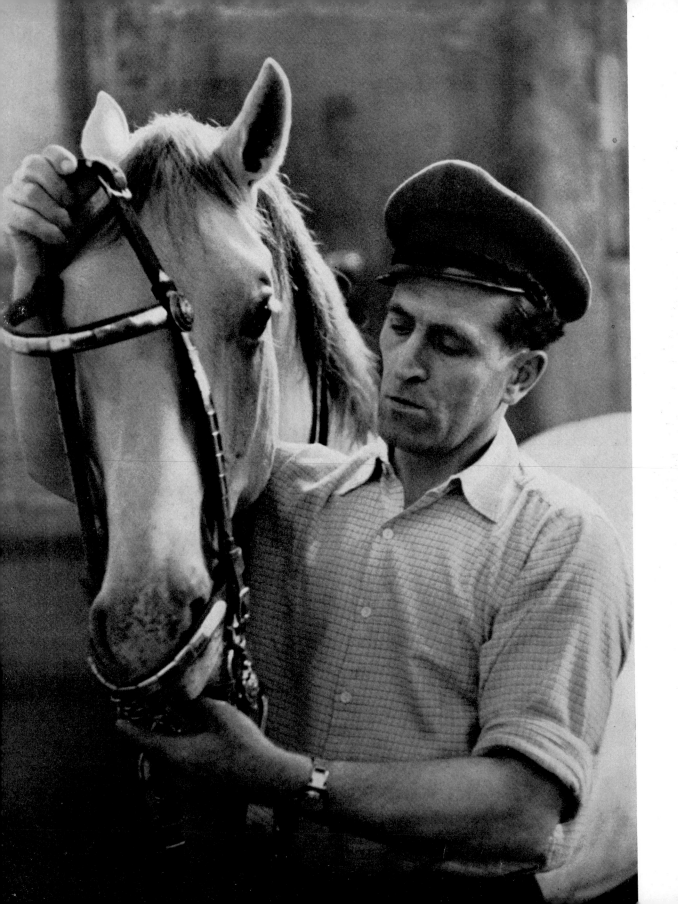

32 *Siglavy Monterosa in a snaffle waiting for the performance "On the long rein"*

Bridling is done calmly and efficiently

33, 34 *Pluto Theodorosta, who was ridden by Queen Elizabeth II in London, above in the gala bridle for the school performance, right in the double bridle ready for the daily training*

35 *Maestoso Alea
in the gala
bridle*

36 *The training of the young stallion begins on the longe*

37, 38 *He must learn to find his balance in all paces*

39 Only the fully
trained stallion
is ridden in a
double bridle.
Pluto Theo-
dorosta

40 The entire
training is
done in a
snaffle. Con-
versano Oma

41　*The basic training of the Lipizzaners is exactly the same as that of any riding horse. Young stallion at the walk*

42　*At the halt the stallion is waiting motionless for the commands of his rider. Pluto The*
　　dorosta in Dublin, 1950

43   *A young stallion at a lively trot*

44 *The moment of suspension at the trot when none of the four legs touches the ground.*
Favory Stornella III

45 *Maestoso Alea at an extended trot during a dressage test in Dortmund, Germany, 1954*

46 *Neapolitano Africa in the spotlights of the White City stadium in London, 1949*

47 *Neapolitano Africa at a halt, fully attentive to his rider, 1948*

48 *Young stallion at a canter*

49 *Maestoso Alea is limbering up at a lively canter for the performance in Hambu*
    Germany, 1951

50   *The school stallion Favory Stornella IV at a collected canter, 1942*

51   *Maestoso Alea at a collected canter, 1955*

54 Maestoso Mercurio
in a half pass to the
right, 1961

55 Maestoso Alea in tʰ
transition to the eˣ
tended trot, 1955

56 *Maestoso Alea at an extended trot, 1957*

57 *Maestoso Alea in the moment of suspension at the extended trot, 195*

58 *Neapolitano Africa in Schloss Wenkenhof in Riehen, Switzerland, 1948*

59 *Maestoso Alea in a piaffe in London, 1953*

60 *Favory Montenegra in a*
    piaffe, 1934

61 *Neapolitano Africa*
    in a piaffe in East
    Burnham Park,
    England, 1949

2   *Siglavy Bona in a piaffe, 1961*

63   *Pluto Presciana II in a piaffe, 1942*

65   *Maestoso Alea performing a piaffe in the beautiful riding hall in Vienna, 1957*

66 *Conversano Bonavista in a passage, 1942*

67   *Conversano Nobila in a passage in Verden/Aller, Germany, 1939*

68   *Pluto Theodorosta in a passage in Wels, Austria, 1951*

69 *Neapolitano Africa in a passage in the Lainzer Park, Vienna, 1944*

70 *Neapolitano Africa in a passage in Frankfurt, Germany, 1950*

71 *Maestoso Alea in a passage, 1957*

72 *Pluto Theodorosta performing the passage on the curb only. Cologne, Germany, 1951*

73 *Neapolitano Africa in a piaffe, ridden on the curb only. Salzburg, 1*

74 Maestoso Alea in a passage, 1957

75 Maestoso Alea in a passage, 19

Beginning of work in hand. Favory Brezovica, 1942

Maestoso Alea in the transition from the trot to the passage, 1957

78   Favory Stornella IV in a piaffe in hand, 1943

79   Favory Stornella II in a piaffe in the pillars, 19.

80 *Conversano Stornella in a levade in hand in the Lainzer Park, 1942*

81 *Conversano Stornella in a levade between the pillars, 19.*

82   *The bay Lipizzaner Neapolitano Ancona in a levade in hand, 1955*

83   *Favory Suleika in a levade in hand in Stockholm, 19*

84   *Favory Suleika in a levade in hand in New York, 1950*

85   *Favory Suleika in a levade between the pillars, 19*

86 *Favory Suleika in a levade in hand. From the film "Vanished Vienna", 1951*

87 *Conversano Stornella in a levade, Vienna, 1934*

88 *Neapolitano Adriana in
a levade, 1928*

89 *Conversano Stornella in
a levade, 1934*

91 *Neapolitano Adriana in a levade, 1928*

Conversano Savona in a levade, 1942

93 *Pluto Brezia is being taught the courbette*

Pluto Brezia preparing to take off for the courbette, 1955

95 *Siglavy Brezovica in the courbette in hand in Hamburg, Germany, 1951*

4 *Siglavy Brezovica in the courbette in hand, 1942*

98 *Pluto Brezia in the courbette in hand, 1955*

99   *Conversano Brezovica in the courbette, 1924*

101 *Siglavy Morella in the courbette, 1962*

Favory Stornella I in the courbette in the Lainzer Park, 1942

103 Neapolitano Santuzza in the ballotade in hand, 1955

105 *Neapolitano Santuzza in the ballotade in hand, 1955*

106 *Neapolitano Santuzza in the ballotade in hand, Stockholm, 1952*

107 *Neapolitano Santuzza in the ballotade in hand, 1*

108   *Neapolitano Santuzza in the ballotade in hand, London, 1953*

110 *Favory Calais in the capriole in hand, St Martin, Austria, 1945*

111 *An exercise rarely seen: Favory Calais in a capriole between the pillars, Lainzer Park,*
1944

112 *Neapolitano Santuzza in the capriole in hand, Berlin, 1958*

113 Neapolitano Santuzza in the capriole in hand, Stockholm, 1952

114　Neapolitano Santuzza in the capriole in hand, Madrid, 1954

116 *Neapolitano Santuzza in the capriole in hand, 1955*

5 *Favory Calais in the capriole in hand, Wels, Austria, 1948*

118 *Favory Stornella III in the capriole under the rider, 1945*

7 *Neapolitano Santuzza in the capriole in hand, 1957*

120   The levade in hand is one of the figurines of Vienna porcelain

9   *The proud stallion Conversano Bonavista posing*
for the famous sculptor Fritz Behn, 1943

121 *The Lipizzaners on tour, boarding the ship to the United States in 1950*

122 *Return to Vienna after an absence of over ten years, 1955*

123 The first trip abroad after the Second World War was to Thun, Switzerland, in 1948

125　*The fortress Hohensalzburg overlooking the quadrille*

4　Performances during the Salzburg Festival, 1950 to 1955

126 *The Lipizzaners in the Piazza di Siena in Rome, 1949*

127 *Performance in Aachen, Germany, 1953*

128 *The Lipizzaners preparing for the performance in Toronto, Canada, 1950*

129 In the time-honoured riding hall of the royal palace Christiansborg in Copenhagen, 1951

130 *From the Olympic Games in Helsinki experts from all over the world came to Stockholm to admire the quadrille of the Spanish Riding School in 1952*

131 *Salute to de La Guérinière in Paris, 1952*

132 *The white stallions entering the show grounds in Hanover, Germany, 19*

133　*Performance of the Lipizzaners in the newly erected stadium in Dortmund, Germany, 1953*

135   *Journey to the land of their ancestors. The Lipizzaners in Seville . . .*

136   *. . . and Barcelona, Spain, 1954*

137   *Farewell to Wels after ten years of exile, 1955*

138 *Colonel Podhajsky announcing the return of the Spanish Riding School to Vienna to the President of Austria, October 26th, 1955 . . .*

139 ...*a historic moment in the riding hall that is so rich in tradition*

140 *The international press is present. Bottom right: Mr Armstrong-Jones, now Lord Snowdon, as photographer. See photograph 33*

141 Performing the Pas de Trois from the left: Conversano Benvenuta, Maestoso Alea, and Conversano Plutona

142 *The enchanting harmony of the movements in the Pas de Trois*

144 ... in a passage,

3 On the long rein: Siglavy Monterosa at a trot ...

145 ...at a
collect-
ed can-
ter.

146 ...a
in a
piaff

148   *The traditional salute*

47   *Solemnly the riders enter for the School quadrille*

149 *And now the white stallions begin to dance*

150 *Renvers in the quadrille*

153 Half pass to the right at
the trot

154, 155 *The figures of the quadrille remind us of the horse ballets of bygone days*

156   *In a film the Lipizzaners were shown as porcelain statues come to life*

157   *As if reflected in a mirror the stallions move towards each other*

159 In the traditional salute the hat is doffed to the painting of Emperor Charles VI

160 *Pluto Theodorosta at the end of the performance, 1955*

161 Shoulder-in in Walt Disney's film "The Miracle of the White Stallions", 1962. The
riders wear the traditional red gala uniform

162 *Shoulder-in on either side of the center line in a quadrille of twelve riders*

163 *Half pass to the left at the trot*

164 Formation of the riders in a passage at the end of the quadrille

165 By his unrestricted confidence in his rider, Maestoso Mercurio proves the correctness
     of his training, 1962

166 *After the daily training Pluto Theodorosta comes for his reward, 1955*

167 *Neapolitano Strana, too, is given his due*

168 *After work, the stallions crossing a busy street to return to their stable*

169   *Conversano Plutona watching the cleaning of the tack*

170   *After the daily wo*

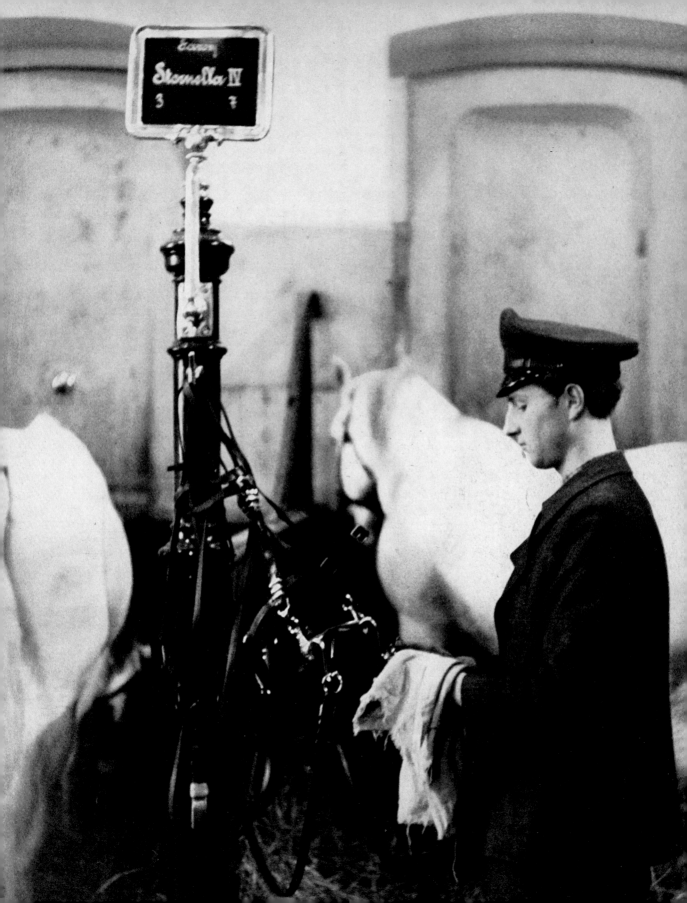

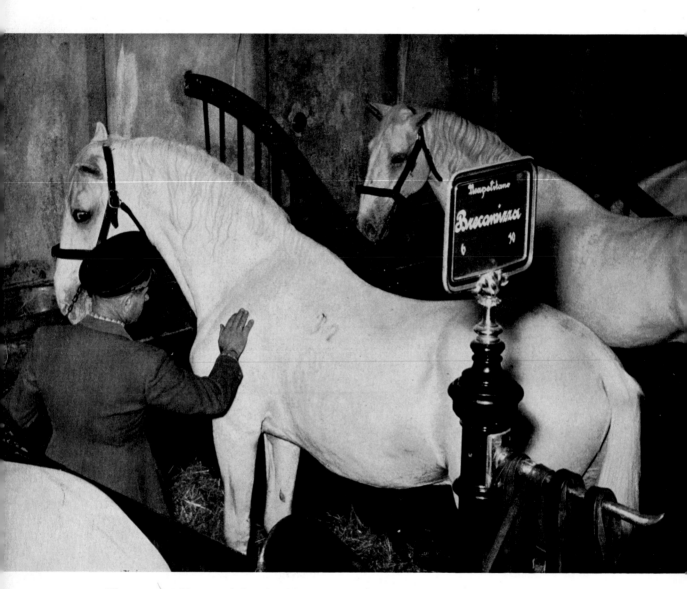

171   *The young stallions and the school horses stand in tie-stalls*

172   *Siglavy Bona, full of confidence, approaching his groom*

173 *Favory Kitty in his stall at feeding time*

174 *In the stables*

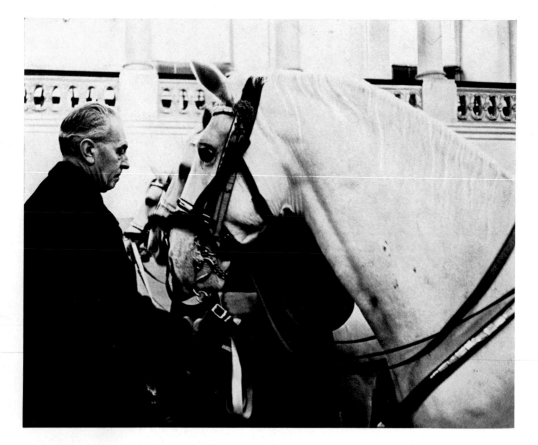

175   *Adieu*